T0114950

SPELLS OF SOLEMN SONGS
POEMS

Kraftgriots

Also in the series (POETRY)

David Cook et al: *Rising Voices*
Olu Oguibe: *A Gathering Fear;* winner, 1992 All Africa Okigbo prize for Literature
     & Honourable mention, 1993 Noma Award for Publishing in Africa
Nnimmo Bassey: *Patriots and Cockroaches*
Okinba Launko: *Dream-Seeker on Divining Chain*
Onookome Okome: *Pendants,* winner, 1993 ANA/Cadbury poetry prize
Nnimmo Bassey: *Poems on the Run*
Ebereonwu: *Suddenly God was Naked*
Tunde Olusunle: *Fingermarks*
Joe Ushie: *Lambs at the Shrine*
Chinyere Okafor: *From Earth's Bedchamber*
Ezenwa-Ohaeto: *The Voice of the Night Masquerade,* joint-winner, 1997 ANA/
     Cadbury poetry prize
George Ehusani: *Fragments of Truth*
Remi Raji: *A Harvest of Laughters,* joint-winner 1997 ANA/Cadbury poetry prize
Patrick Ebewo: *Self-Portrait & Other Poems*
George Ehusani: *Petals of Truth*
Nnimmo Bassey: *Intercepted*
Joe Ushie: *Eclipse in Rwanda*
Femi Oyebode: *Selected Poems*
Ogaga Ifowodo: *Homeland & Other Poems,* winner, 1993 ANA poetry prize
Godwin Uyi Ojo: *Forlorn Dreams*
Tanure Ojaide: *Delta Blues and Home Songs*
Niyi Osundare: *The Word is an Egg* (2000)
Tayo Olafioye: *A Carnival of Looters* (2000)
Ibiwari Ikiriko: *Oily Tears of the Delta* (2000)
Arnold Udoka: *I am the Woman* (2000)
Akinloye Ojo: *In Flight* (2000)
Joe Ushie: *Hill Songs* (2000)
Ebereonwu: *The Insomniac Dragon* (2000)
Deola Fadipe: *I Make Pondripples* (2000)
Remi Raji: *Webs of Remembrance* (2001)
'Tope Omoniyi: *Farting Presidents and Other Poems* (2001)
Tunde Olusunle: *Rhythm of the Mortar* (2001)
Abdullahi Ismaila: *Ellipsis* (2001)
Tayo Olafioye: *The Parliament of Idiots: Tryst of the Sinators* (2002)
Femi Abodunrin: *It Would Take Time: Conversation with Living Ancestors* (2002)
Nnimmo Bassey: *We Thought It Was Oil But It Was Blood* (2002)
Ebi Yeibo: *A Song For Tomorrow and Other Poems* (2003)
Adebayo Lamikanra: *Heart Sounds* (2003)
Ezenwa-Ohaeto: *The Chants of a Minstrel* (2003), winner, 2004 ANA/NDDC poetry
     prize and joint-winner, 2005 LNG The Nigeria Prize for Literature
Seyi Adigun: *Kalakini: Songs of Many Colours* (2004)

SPELLS OF SOLEMN SONGS
POEMS

Khabyr Fasasi

kraftgriots

Published by
Kraft Books Limited
6A Polytechnic Road, Sango, Ibadan
Box 22084, University of Ibadan Post Office
Ibadan, Oyo State, Nigeria
✆ +234803 348 2474, 805 129 1191
E-mail: kraftbooks@yahoo.com
www.kraftbookslimited.com

© Khabyr Fasasi, 2015

First published 2015

ISBN 978–978–918–324–1

= KRAFTGRIOTS =
(A literary imprint of Kraft Books Limited)

All Rights Reserved

First printing, September 2015

Dedication

To

the bearers of the agonies of cursed leadership
the hands and voices working and bursting for the purity
of this space

Acknowledgements

Many thanks to:

The womb,
my co-travellers

Contents

Dedication 5
Acknowledgements 6

Entrance **9**
Entrance 10
I came 12
I am (I) 13
I am (II) 14
Rags bind me 15

Chase the fox... .... **17**
Think of 18
Survival 20
Wailing seasons 21
And the cat looked back 23
Slave's errands 25
Of eggs and mountain 28
Cants from the rock 29
Mouth pad 32
Houseflies 33
Have you seen? 34
Sleaze 35
Our sweat their wealth 36
Eat the world (I) 38
Eat the world (II) 39
The dog woofs 40
Payback 42
Death to the bastards 44

Love you not 45
Fetid farts 48
Insipid okro soup 50
Acting placards 52
Tell me miracles 54
Idols on altars 55
Booze thralldom 57
Song of the sadist 60

Face the fowl... .... **61**
Stand up you 62
Here 64
Successful 66
Natal kneeling 68
The womb 70
One white witch 71
Said she 73
Stumps 74
Says the spirit 75
The journey 77
Life dialectics 78
Life is 80
The bell 81
Sweet sorrow 82
Your planet 83

Entrance

I solemnly seek
Let me be welcome …

Entrance

Entrance I solemnly seek
Into the lean land of the learned
Into the finest legion of the gifted pen-bred
Accept the exploits of my shaky palms
And the sudden strides of my soles

Entrance I solemnly seek
Into the grand sanctuary of shrewd eloquence
May I wine with wonderful weavers of raw words
Into iridescent colours and shapes
As refined symphony above seasons

Entrance I solemnly seek
Into the muffled minds of placid men
Whose eyes have borne blinding absurdity
But still squeeze the golden silence
Till torn in riotous innards
Bitter constrictions choke their gullets
And oceans of censure spew out stifled scorn

Entrance I solemnly seek
Let my voice be airily wafted
Into tasteless and sealed auricles
Let my breath clear the serene path
Into dark jungles of tangled minds

Entrance I solemnly seek
Annoyance, the path to wretch,
Blind rage, this day I banish your vagrant fury
Let them who swallowed you
Secrete you in speedy sweats and wastes
And hastily strive to lick my velvety tongue

Entrance I solemnly seek
Let ears in raptures wait on my lines
Let the breaths between my labials be pondered
For deafened oral perceptions soon lose astute counsel
Steal from my tongue and fashion into sun
Steal my breath and make the radiant moon
Whatever I weave novelty at your touch

Entrance I solemnly seek
Smooth and unhindered entrance
For stumps do not deter the serpent's voyage
The jungle does not hinder the squirrel's passage
The love of honey displaces all diets
The sight of birds brings dimples to children's cheeks
The new born appears painting happiness on visages

Entrance I solemnly seek
With resonant rhymes and swaying reasons
Home and abroad friends of rain
None wishes rainfall as foe
Entrance I solemnly seek
Into the lean land of eloquence

With glee let me be welcome …

I came

I came here
Holding a bundle of naivety
   Lost my naivety
    In abrupt terror
      Lost my terror
      In ropy inquisition
        Lost my inquisition
        In ugly recognition
          Lost my recognition
          In mint of wisdom
Wisdom I grasped in the wilderness of the world.

I am (I)

I am a wordsmith
I bend and unbend, mend and smooth out lyrical lines
I craft nectar out of the crooked crock
I must not keep words locked up in my throat
Who should find free sway
In radiant rhymes and sound reasons
Lest I grow protruding oesophagus
And starve the world of decency.

I am a wandering minstrel
I must not tarry for long in mother's womb
Nor brood over tidal thoughts in isolation
I must trek my songs to far-flung lands
Lest the words bottled within and within
Accumulate into a bursting ball
Of insane inconveniences for her succour.

I am a brainy bard
Parrots, pigeons and sparrows breathe in me
In constant pronouncements of virtues
I feast on feats and legendary
Fuel and flourish my unique standard
Eons my tongue recalled and chewed
Into the present to chart the morrow
And silence names me the noise of yesteryears.

I am a rhymester
Rhythm of honeyed labials and velvety voice
Raining gently into discerning lobes
Raping the rage of spells of retches
Inaugurating drizzling reason nonpareil in place of rage
That rhythmic reason may reign in riches.

I am (II)

I am the somnolent bed from which ku ku ruu ku wakes them
I am the haven they turn to with the receding sun

I am the hearth whose eyes bear the red-hot heat
As spiralling smoke and sweat seized the atmosphere
That mouths may munch and bellies bulge with rations

I am the dug garbage bin, sanctuary of filths and secrets
The latrine they ceaselessly praise with sputum
For relieving gaits and facades of stinking burdens

I am the imposing fortress fending them off
From fear, vermin and vanity

I am the safe pulse that keeps secrets in lodges
The dirty hearts run here to conceal pathetic riddles

I am the expansive refuge they run to
When shredded hearts seek solace
In me they sleep away their undone dreams

I am the somnolent bed from which ku ku ruu ku wakes them
I am the haven they turn to with the receding sun

Rags bind me

Rags bind me to the roads of rigour
Rejection strengthens my feeble bones
Leaning nose-to-nose with the lowly
Sharing the crumbs, pains and forlorn fates
On dejected streets of loneliness
I draw my strengths from the joy that I am me.

Baked in the scorching sun by day
And drenched by the eroding rains of May
I trekked on broomstick legs, infirm on proud poles of mine
The fearful feathers and shrieking owls tortured me
In the night of scorching days
Like a serene massif I come to light
Holding on to the fort of nature in me.

In the hoofed ranch or dusty tang
With putrid reeks of decayed fodder and dung
Or blinding and bitter taste of mephitic ether
I stretched forth from foul and toxin
Gazing into the futility of the deadly affluent
Dying to pillage and pile up expensive poisons,
And paying for luxurious rags and reeks.

And rags bind me to the fuzzy vision of life
Yet I stretched forth to flourish on the idiom:
Even when the fire dances its bloodthirsty dance
The wise dances gently on survival pace.

... looting our lands,
   looting our values,
     looting our eyes,
      looting our minds ...

Chase the fox ...

     Chase the fox ...
      fight the fox
       with sticks and spittle,
        with brains and brawns,
         with brooms and blazing breaths ...

Think of ...

Think of your words,
Muffled by mum nose
Obnoxious crinkling of gaping holes

Your words
That reminded your stinks
Of its inaugural dirtiness

Your words
That tingled the bogus truth
To recall its lurid lies

Think of
The pregnant noise
Lurking in the womb of still silence

Think of
The raucous rage
Hiding behind brimming smiles

Think of
The fatal venom
In the white veins of sweet salt

Think of
The violent 'no!'
Behind every syrupy 'yes'

Think of
Beyond the shining faces
Into the bitterness of black bellies

Think of
Your turning back
To see your paid supporters petered out

Think of
Before and after
Think of now ...

Survival

The partridge ponders ...
Thanks to the farmer who tends his farm
Thanks to the one who tends not his farm
Daily I feed safely in the bushy farm
Nightly I sleep safely in the tended farm
Feed feed flap my feathers
Watch watch waggles my wit.

The pullet portends ...
Mother had pointed out
Roam the separate paths not
Hawks and vultures protect their progeny
But prosper by hawking prompt passing
To straying posterity of others
Pleasant entrails their pleasurable repasts.

The pig pleads ...
I'm not pleased with such a play
As slap-my-rump-I-slap-your-rump
Slap my rump a pleasant slap
I cry khum, khum, khum, khum
Pack a painful punch to the pouch
A positive passage to perdition.

Wailing seasons

the smoky rickety truck on this dry and rough road
trudging rowdily on and on to no destination
pulling passengers left and low on aimless wheels
whooshing sweltering winds of blazing smoke
darker than the dark womb of chimneys to
harmattaned flora and fauna: elements tilting against hope
at the mercy of death to hot tides of burning waves
waves standing tall to harass the roofed belly of heavens,
the sky belches frequently from the furnace of offensives
till perforated, heavens shed hot showers drenching and
drowning dwellers

the night soil man on duty perfumed self in scenting shits
and his penchant for generosity drew him to soil
the sacred space in loads of pungencies in the name of
helping his space, having donated the best he has
but the clean space knows that his perfume is poison
yet the bird, barren of hope, against will and wits
perched precariously on the dangling string of death
itself and its thoughtless head dangling to and fro,
elusive is the name of peace to the line and tactless bird
sorrow down below is saddened sorrow hung on
the erratic rock

the stench from poisoned hearts to fermented breaths
strongly stood spiral, awkwardly straight
forcefully annexing and choking holes, hoods, huts, houses
till punctured and defenceless, the resilient space stinks
stench from bitter decay, dungeoned darkness,
maggots in millions, bitterness expelling taste and blinding
sights
crawls on kinked claws in the darkness of the sunny day

the clouds in fear run off its silver lining, the moon retreats
into its traceless ball and the sun, ruined, banishes its ray to
ruin the space

cold, cold, cruelly cold like the nose of the rabid dog
cold, apathetically cold even in this hunting season
the steel heart, frozenly cold, refuses to melt its ice
to permit the penetration of warm sense and sane reason
into drearily cold and closed recesses
unseeing sights, deaf lobes and muted minds
on legs squeezing through the path of blighted abyss
and dispersing callous coldness to green hearts of millions
then cold pulse beats from petulant hearts to veins
irascibility read boldly on haggard faces on hungry streets
impatience with all: living and gone, and with self now
the fad

but fire in the strong veins of the majestic *iroko*, burning
and burning, arresting the lion heart of the giant
who now rears back and runs away from self,
seeking shelter in the acrid lamina of the bitter leaf
where lies safety for the bold heart? For the bitter leaf?
one a giant eremite, the other a flimsy chew by the sheep
all dread the fiery doom whose answers beg the question,
the rumpus of fury beyond the mighty and midget
beyond saintly experience and doused not by the dove
or the soothing balm of the snail, raging and consuming
the distressed core of spineless fatalists walking
with corpses

fierily cold stench of the night soil man on bumpy wheels
devours the jagged green universe like
greased lightning like colonies
of famished termites
on the wood

And the cat looked back

What did the cat say as he looked back?
When you dried off his wetness
And gave him warmth by the fireside
And bid him farewell in warm weather
After a grateful tongue has licked lukewarm milk
And steps away from you he looked back
What did the cat say?

What did the cat say as he looked back?
When you caged him for empty agonizing stretch
Without a faint guilt or fear of green
And you arrived to see his pale and peeling frame
And steps away from you he looked back
With staggering gait sustaining staggering sights
What did the cat say?

What did the cat say as he looked back?
When you wield your rod of rough conduct
When you breathe down broad necks, and sit on gaunt spines
And you cover yourself in stolen fur, the cat's birthright
And you skinned the cat of his inheritance
And steps away from you he looked back
With distrust and hate howling on his forsaken face
What did the cat say?

What did the cat say as he looked back?
When the million minds and trunks, turned blanks and bones,
Crawled constantly, clanking raucously for rightful revenge
Meowing feebly on sickly frames to your fort
And steps away they looked at you
Aware that swollen, larger-than-life Krahnian Doe
Once crawled and meowed lamely in a stump

What did the cat say?

What did the cat say as he looked back at you?
Meowed, yowled or growled?
After your hands have doled out to the world
Wailed, whimpered or chattered?
The crushing hammer of your soiled heart,
Purred, caterwauled or screeched?

What did the cat say as he looked back?

Slave's errands

The stretched splashy triad sent me on a slave's errand
Errand I must deliver like a picture-perfect well-bred
The natural marine confluence of diverse-fused parts
Warns 'let the clans I locked together by my rippling tongues
Be so tranquilly locked and constantly lubricated
For whoever thinks otherwise shall stray away without a trace
Devoid of tranquil lubricant in harsh harmattan'.

The treasure-trove of the house of *Aje* sent me on a slave's errand
Errand I must deliver like a picture-perfect well-bred
Juicy beverage, you grab and gnaw, raw or refined,
Wealth from forests, grasslands and flowing waters
Caution 'let the souls in this house beware
Your wealth of attachment is your wealth of sustenance
Pull apart is straitened sustenance
Penury shall plaster your hamlets and pockets of division'.

The illustrious ancestors sent me on a slave's errand
Errand I must deliver like a picture-perfect well-bred
The long gory ropes that fastened together this solidity
That saw the first honeyed nectars of daybreak
Assert 'let no offspring, on any ruse, treachery or avarice,
Beat the drum of war or sing the song of severance
Like the scattered and strayed children of the serpent
Else, you shall have no home or source left as yours
See, the hawks are impatiently waiting to swoop on you
And our sweats and blood shall have run for naught'.

The unstifled civil martyrs sent me on a slave's errand
Errand I must deliver like a picture-perfect well-bred
The resonating roars from the dead ransom, urgently

Echo and echo 'let the laboured but lost souls
Be comforted by the pleasing recompense in your union
For on moulding that pillar of oneness we petered out:
Unite the flock our charge, break away our wrath'.

The crippled tides and butchered growth sent me on a slave's
errand
Errand I must deliver like a picture-perfect well-bred
The agonized flora and fauna of the swampy creeks
Cry to heavens 'let fair long throats who gash and gore our
purity,
Let hawks within who roam about in stolen ruptured eyes
Be ready for sudden overrun: purblind and choked throats'.

The dirty dove guarded in green sent me on a slave's errand
Errand I must deliver like a picture-perfect well-bred
After all the dirt and tears thrown ceaselessly at purity
Pure peace appealed 'let the precarious insignia stand firm
on souls
And the tattered flag be renewed and groomed in hearts
For I project your amity and unified fertility
As direction, as insurance for your morrow
Lose your ensign, you lose your morrow
Lose your insignia, you lose your name'.

The dirt, deaths and disillusionment sent me on a slave's
errand
Errand I must deliver like a picture-perfect well-bred
Noxious eyesores, derangement and deaths roused
ceaselessly
By the stony hands of the conceited political tricksters
Swore 'let such dusts, dirt, deaths and disillusionment be
hurled
In hasty unity, with all limbs, at the crafty but frightened
faces of fraudsters
Let memories of these devious cheats be swept off our sane

space
And the ugly bane and infections of bugle blowers be blotted out'.

The massive circumference sent me on a slave's errand
Errand I must deliver like a picture-perfect well-bred
Standing on the broad shoulders of Africa, the strong tower
Thundered 'let this rugged rock be fissured by none, high or low
That loafing lizards of foreign terrain may hibernate not
Bunch your rank together like broomsticks and brush away
The greedy and gluttonous goons in government'.

---

* *Aje:* A Yoruba deity of commerce and wealth.

Of eggs and mountain

Eggs my eyes have seen
Eggs from feathers and crawlers
Eggs my eyes have seen
Soft and hard cracks.

Eggs my eyes have not seen
In hundreds or legions
Rashly incited and egged on
Clad in armours and marching forth
Towards the serenely sitting massif
Rockily ready for raid or reunion.

Whose line loses life and wins loss?
If not the heartless shell-shielded legions
Eggy shells of tenuous ovals but
Scrappy cracks on hitting the rocky shell

Whose foolishness is bewailed
In the loss of right and reason?
Whose future is shattered
In the loss of legions and posterity?

Who else sits rockily on triumph?
Than the sturdy and steady giant
Imposing patience serenely sitting on peace.

Cants from the rock

I have been served lies, demeaning lies from the topmost
rock
'I promise visionary and committed leadership.'
The vision of the blind in the dark caves within
For sights to be sights, apparition and fragrant phantasm,
Cobweb of wool must be cast off blurred vision.
Devotion can dance luminously on lips even when
indifference
Writes actions in bold, when hesitant strides celebrate apathy
I have heard enough cant, manifest cant, crumbling cant.

I have been fed by the first mouth enough surges of humbugs
'I am committed to ensuring public safety and security.'
With poor police officers of the roadsides, regular
mendicants,
Vulnerable, save disused civil war metals of multiple rusts
Force forced to stand the sophistry of armed wizards as if
Blood runs not in their sapped and poverty-trained veins...
With abductions that propel outlaws onto the throne of tin
gods
And Saharan seizure by the dissidents of doves and faith
Feed me no more cant, flagrant cant, crumbling security
cant.

Tokenistic pledges from the faint voice waft into my drooping
ears
'I will fight corruption and demand transparency...'
With state pardons and pledges for crowned corruption
Wretches who displayed their home for an open market sale
Still dine on the narrowed national neck. Three airfields!
The fleet in the backyard of the rock. Six hundred men!
Escort abroad to debate heavens, earth and beyond

When attendants party nonstop in who-dare-question-me
sleaze
Demand transparency from the near-by burglars, butchers
and goons
Ask your grasping flight and oil officers if you dare
Ask the retinue of barren long-throats before this.
Enough of empty cant, cant of worms, crumbling cant.

Easy to be all mouth, mouthing galling two-facedness
'I am focused on addressing our infrastructure needs'
Phony pledges for ages falling on decrepit infrastructure
Focused to pull down universities and compos mentis
Focused to pinion the long arms of painfully red roads
Speedily handing deteriorating deaths to sickly clinics
Flickering fluctuant of voltage as erratic as Abiku's eyelids
One wormy snail on the noisy rail of benumbed death
Too much cant, deafening cant of irritants

I have seen froth falling from both sides of a reeking mouth
'I commit myself to doing my very best...'
The best of state protection to rogues and fraudulent bastards
The best of neglect to the crying roads of life
The best of apathy to the masses' cry of deprivation
The very best of lethargy to constant abuse by multinationals
Firm and very best in foreign travels, anemic to native
concerns.
The best of efficient cant, sincerely committed to free-flowing
cant.

Lip-servicing fraud, each lie firmly saddling another
Lies on lies like the trust cats vow to generations of mice
'We are fighting corruption in all facets...and we are
succeeding'
When we ordered new governors to let sleeping dogs lie
To throw all thoughts of probe into the trash can of blanks

When we plucked out EFCC's fangs, and made ICPC prowls
blindly
When we plastered fetid wounds of fraud with national
medals
When we beam well-done smiles from the rock at frauds
Then we have succeeded, won the wars against corruption
Corrupt cant! Tall tales! Lies on lies on lies!

I have heard oaths promised in the name of hell
'I promise to give my all, my best...'
I give my all ...to me; give my naught ...to all
I throw out some sour slop – my finest best – to starved
indigent
I take all from my naught and I sit my best on subsidy ruse
Where the lives of civil subsidy is robbed in big billions
With my all, I'm all free to roam the cosmos
With my all, I grant you good representation in the world
With my all, the world sees your rare luxury in me
Even if poverty ravages the swamps, savannahs and cities.
My finest best, my shameful all is all, all is all.
Clap out cant! Clap out crafty cant!

Mouth pad

Defending the foul-falling frothy shit, this sham
on the tactless tongue of the unpolished narcissist
yeoman yearning for trust in blatant hoax
in guise of jaw-breakers thicker than thesaurus, but
noxious sham of yours are toxic pollutants to this space.

Old log of wood hijacking the blazing mike
killing and sealing the dream of previously singed silver
upon the squalid alter of a lost loner
payback is as near as the nightfall,
engulfing hastily, like the honourable shame from baba.

Houseflies

hordes of houseflies are on the prowl
soaring high supplying dirt and diseases
taking forceful charge of the sound space
till settled loutishly, with infectious wings
on the luscious honey pot at the centre
slurping the stolen sweet supplies of bees
licking the loot with proboscis into bulging bellies
lapping it up with limbs and weighty wings
recklessly rejecting rational cries for restraint
snubbing sound sounds of the strap
breathing from bloated behind
till dead drunk, death dims their minds
and no trace of their names,
      of their ruins
         remains

Have you seen?

Have you seen
the master weaver of webs
from the ancient network of tissues
superb builder of spiraling aesthetics
sly spinner of the peacock loom?

Have you seen
the hanging mansion
splendour surpassing all splendour
fine fabrics on footless foundation
steady snare of sticky silk
on scaffold of unseen strands?

Have you seen
the lord of the octagon
in his palace of gold and growth
relishing the most royal repasts
enmeshing ill-omened delicacies
for his bulbous buttocks and swollen stomach?

Alas! Have you seen
how a flimsy bunch of brooms
pronounced prompt ruling on
the scaffold, strand, spiralling stronghold
and the most excellent lord of vanity
all in a clean sweeping swoop?

Have you seen
the emptiness that trails
the flimsiness of the bulbous lord
and his empire of mighty mirage?

Sleaze

A long crooked snake
poisoning the public purse
crawling up the criminal's crotch
venom of climbers up to the bulging belly
up to the fleshy occipital bone
and up poisoning the airy arteries and veins.

A sly spleen of sane senses
sweet sour serrations of reasons.
the one pit where business crooks queue with clergies
on the cluttered heels of con and cunt swap
cleared by tensed and brain-dead politicians.

A wild fire engulfing the core of the civil slaves
hot leads from burning hands
creeping mullishly unto flaming mouths and rumbling
bellies.
A bursting blood that runs in the core of all
up and down, left and ill
like a circus of viral infections.

Our sweat their wealth

Brazen seals of sleaze on political foreheads
Our sweats their wealth

Pauperizing public properties for private pouches
Our sweats their wealth

Fuel subsidy savings in billions vamoosed
Our sweats their wealth

Oil wells partitioned by venal hauling away the nation
Our sweats their wealth

Trendy limos limitless from loots
Our sweats their wealth

Dandy dresses shipped with costly vanity
Our sweats their wealth

Senators sitting heavily on enacted wealth
Our sweats their wealth

Fleet of flights the docile head's help
Our sweats their wealth

Judicial defense of verity is falsehood nairaed
Our sweats their wealth

Desperate fights to hem in our stable heads
Our sweats their wealth

Bent backs of slavish serfs of wealth
Our sweats their wealth

Squawking voices of hectic hecklers
Our sweats their wealth

Sickening clinics for the slogging masses
Our sweats their wealth

Foreign hospitalization for frenzied felons
Our sweats their wealth

Tearing our unity to evade one thrashing voice
Our sweats their wealth

In the midst of tension, terror and rift, they crave
Our sweats their wealth.

Eat the world (I)

Hear the shameful chants
falling off the fool's mouth
like droppings in urgent refrains
I shall eat this world!

Hear the drunk's tottering dance
swaying paces of upturned brain,
the derisible dance in the open market
I shall eat this world!

Your old man sang same
and his father who bore him
in bogus garments of the gourds
gone now your father's father
foaming in froth
with drooling lips, purring
I shall eat this world!

Eat the world (II)

Gone the beaut
gone the maiden that bore your mother
younger and brighter in early days
nectar of blooms in early rains
gold and silver they overly made
connections to the firmament their fancy
I shall eat this world!

To the arm of time
all lost,
short and lost
foregoers and all,
short and lost to time,
lost!
for none is as long as time
I shall eat this world!

Intoxicated at his adornment
And hastily running
after his lures
Or waits and watches
its ornamental thrills
I shall eat this world!

Alas!
The world clutches,
chews,
and sheds
that shrivelling leaf
off its branch
I shall eat ...

The dog woofs!

The dog woofs! 'People come and see ...'
The dog barks! 'People come and see ...
How they plunder their humanity
How *animans* excellently impoverish their homes
Even when they brag that sanity sleeps at their doors
That wisdom is locked up in their pouches.'

The dog woofs! 'People come and see ...'
The dog barks! 'People come and see ...
Same blood and same cord they are
Same tongue and same soul they are
Sweet smiles in the sparkle of broad days
Caustic crimes in the belly of the night.'

The dog woofs! 'Nations come and see ...'
The dog barks! 'Nations come and see ...
The rapid retrogression they revel in
The accolades they confer on sleazy souls
The chop-and-waste malady they hail
The only ministry all officers oversee.'

The dog woofs! 'The world come and help ...'
The dog barks! 'The world come and help ...
Foolery and buffoonery have taken charge
Rights and reason are exiled to the dung hill
Filthy feet are freely flying about in the firmament
And barren heads are trampling the squalid soil.'

The dog woofs! 'Heavens come and save ...'
The dog barks! 'Heavens come and save ...
Now they spill siblings' blood in the daylight
Like the worshippers of Ogun, the blood bather
As they compete in elections to stamp

Debauched titles and mammon to their null skulls.'

The dog woofs! 'Heavens save my soul!'
The dog barks! 'Heavens save my soul!
Siblings breakfasting on brothers' entrails
Siblings scoffing sisters' innards
Insane horror in the yard of the sanest cannibals,
Yet wisest beyond all crawlers and greenery.

Payback

Your wealth I embezzled
Chokes me in my conscience
Chokie chokie!
That's how it chokes consciences
Chokie chokie!

Your trust I tore to tatters
Tears my integrity in public
Tearie tearie!
That's how it tears integrities
Tearie tearie!

Your rights I wrongfully ate
Churn me in my stomach
Churnie churnie!
That's how it churns stomachs
Churnie churnie!

Your assets I mismanaged
Cause me heartaches
Causie causie!
That's how it causes heartaches
Causie causie!

Your life I impoverished
Gives me nightmares
Givie givie!
That's how it gives nightmares
Givie givie!

The bloody carnage I caused
Snuffs out my precious life
Snuffie snuffie!
That's how it snuffs out lives

Snuffie snuffie!

The limitless lives I snapped
Clasp tight my jugular veins
Claspie claspie!
That's how they clasp jugular veins
Claspie claspie!

Your generations I silently killed
Ask murderously for my blood
Askie askie!
That's how they ask for blood
Askie askie!

Your forgiveness I beg before death
For now I detest death
Beggie beggie!
That's how they beg before death
Beggie beggie!

Taste the bitter bile of your blessing
Taste the tear! Taste your blood!
Tastie tastie!
That's how you taste death!
Tastie tastie!

Death to the bastards!

Let the bastards burn in flames
Burn in the blazing blue infernos
Infernos thirstier than the harmattan fire
Death to the bastards!

These base-worshipping bastards
Ignoble sellers of common heritage
Shameless outsellers of a race
Foolish bargainers with fair hawks
Death to the bastards!

They point to their family heritage
With callous left hands
But rejoice in the foreign netting they wear
Bought from the fair prey
With urined outstretched rights
Death to the bastards!

Who tear our wealth at raucous meetings
Dead minds dead conscience on dead bulk
And scurried for elusive safety in aliens
Building empires from wispy spits
Ah! By the dew are spit empires demolished
And death to the bastards!

Now these dogs, heads excreta-stained
Scamper back to the home they gored
Hurry back to the heritage they betrayed
Hurl! Hurl! Hurl your venomous bile at them!
Rejected within and pursued without
And left with but one choice
Death to the bastards!

Love you not

By love!
They love you not, Nigeria!
Though you sow harmony in their warring hearts
Brought low their differences and unite them on soaring
height
You banish their hunger and contain their insanity
You stand them tall at territories of trepidation
You enrich their affronted tatters and parched pouches
Like ingratitude is their garment, they love you not
Though they sing soaring allegiance to your name

By love!
They love you not, Nigeria!
They pound your drum of growth to tear
They sing your sweet song to vain smugness
They scorch, paw and cut your thick limbs
Kill and burn your brimming blessings
Though your large hands shield them from cold and fear
They churn your stomach as the Jews churn Moses'
They slow down your soaring story
With stale and selfish discourse of departed years

By love!
They love you not, Nigeria!
Politicians, office-holders feeding fat on public purse
Animans feeding ballooned bellies and foreign vaults
Feeding the unborn and nameless future
Aye! Thinning down the masses of workhorse,
The slavish scroungers who truly sustain
The great fort and loft with oozing sweats
In cold and urgent blood in warmth
but hold on to life with nibbles from crumbs and stale snacks

By love!
They love you not, Nigeria!
These crafty business bands sitting comfortably
On your warm shoulders tapping your strength
From the crevices of your rural beds to urban sprawls
Spanking you yet with misery and ruin to flora and fauna
Dispiritedly draining the breath and blood off your seeds
Now they rout and ruin your grassroots from roots
Determined to leave you wretched beyond rectification

By love!
They love you not, Nigeria!
The cultured conquests contrived by your own hands
Demandingly groomed to ingenious giants of high opinions
On different domains now mobile books and brains
Yes, good heads, but folding arms as spectators of your faith
Mum onlookers maintaining let-the-ruin-run-on posture
Those hens know how to protect their growing chicks
But are swift to push yours to death

By love!
They love you not, Nigeria!
Though they claim they can breast death
Defending the strange scrolls on lecterns
Die dealing in thirsty tongues salivating for tithes
Die showing the world they are holier than Christ
But they can lose not a tress of hair
In the name of Christ or their source
They love you not, like they love Christ not
Though they foam this love on smelling sputum

By love!
They love you not, Nigeria!
Though they regal in the glory of serene salaams
Faces filled with olive but hearts squeezing lives to death
They spurn and turn the scrolls upside down

For they stand brainwashed by the jinn
To disperse dissension and put down pacifism
And insist death is the best option of ministration
Reap my reasoning or slump by sword

By love!
They love you not, Nigeria!
Those foreign unfair hawks,
Implacable foes, superficially affable
Opportunists prancing fanatically around planetary pickings
Like legions of ants cowardly coveting cubes of sugar
Vulturine preys awaiting unwary victims at lowest ebbs
To suck up pirated blessings and blood of the land
And throw the rest in burning turmoil
One vision and mission: to thief and throw aflame

By love!
They love you not, Nigeria!
Rash miscreants within and taloned hawks without
But noble name you bestowed on them as your permeating scent
Fame, faith and fortune you offered as symbols of true love
Yet they love you not
I swear by love!
They love you not, Nigeria!

Fetid farts

The turbulent tide courses on
But with fetid farts the sickly sort slurs his thanks

The grinning gap-toothed
pushed up by one-minute martial rebellion
trampled his broad beam on the treasury
close on the heel of a decade draining
quashing fortunes, voices and warm blood
into unquestionable bullets and armoured tanks
and replacing the emptiness with genial smile

The turbulent tide courses on
But with fetid farts the sickly sort slurs his thanks

The enoughy cold-stone, terse
eyes on the nectar craved a short taste
speaking power through the cold steel
tongue on sapping the treasury
crooked fingers pillaging plenteous power
sun-shading brutish blank moods
decreeing stiff fright, force and fatality
to enemies, parrots and friends
thought in mind and seen in dreams
rode to ruin on a 'one-eared' imported mule

The turbulent tide courses on
But with fetid farts the sickly sort slurs his thanks

The sodden shoeless
docile disciple of the certified felon all the while
strikingly out of his gourd
soars high over heads of princes:
what pleasant surprise to hopefuls
and cuts the wounded bull in wasteful chunks

delights in the crumbling of kith and kin
cries from the dead and the living is music
to the horrendous leisure of a heartless despot

Eh! The turbulent tide courses on
But with fetid farts the sickly sort slurs his thanks

Amidst the tidal flow of the strange truth
that blazing fire consumes sodden branches
that hawks someday peck on skulls of kings
We watch the sickly sorts slur thanks with fetid farts
As the turbulent tide courses on

Insipid okro soup

Let him have the insipid okro soup
that hunter who returns without a kill.

that head that grieves for the breath to command simple sanity
that gullet that welcomes good rations of garbage
those canines which have lost the potency to crush
those legs which have lost the strength of routing routes
that penis which lacks the feat of nocturnal doggedness.

Let him have the insipid okro soup
that hunter who returns without a kill.

that gong which has discarded his potency of piercing noise
that law which has lost the power to compel conformity
that head which finds no comfort sitting steadily on the neck
those eyes which never desire to see beyond the nose
the heart which has failed to pump his plasma and passion.

Let him have the insipid okro soup
that hunter who returns without a kill.

that hawk which bewails his wonders of obsessive stealing
that lion which shivers at the thought of stalking and roaring
that peacock whose beauty is a faded reference of yesteryears
that glowworm which mourns the want of its luminous light.

Let him have the insipid okro soup
that hunter who returns without a kill.

that soldier who weakens at the wailing of summoning bugle
that fisherman who grieves with the fear of the deep
that bard whose nightingale's voice has deserted him
that fart which mourns the demise of its disgusting sound
and smell

Let him have the insipid okro soup
that hunter who returns without a kill.

that salt which has forsaken his tempting sweetness
that potash which laments the loss of its biting sourness
that rain which fails to break the soil and cool the space
that rock afraid to crush the raids by eggs on his region.

Let him have the insipid okro soup
That hunter who returns without a kill.

Acting placards

It was yesterday
Some mean men paid peanuts
To some withering wombs
To troop to the streets
Clutching pallid placards on heartless hands
Drowsily driven by lecherous legs
Their grievances?
Leave her alone, the Honourable Minister
She is our dutiful daughter
Nay! She is not corrupt
But generously co-opting
The national free-for-all into her bogus bags
Of pomades, powders and powers of the pussy
No to arrest, no to trial
No to court case
We no go gree ...

The day before ...
Honourable Senator in EFCC's net
His village folks puffed out
Like froth to the streets
Barefooted and famished lot on dusty day
Invoking the Honourable's innocence
Recounting how he laboured hard
Sweating to serve his people
To build scores of structures in Lagos and London,
To erect edifices in Dublin and Dubai,
Abuja and America all in two senatorial years
How he purchased his private jets
From his hard-earned sweats in two senatorial years
How he freely frequents foreign vaults
In the interest of the masses

But abandons his shrivelling village
His scrawny folks say no to the trial
Of a good statesman
No to arrest, no to trial
No to court case
We no go gree ...

And today ...
It is His Excellency,
The governor in graft
Who sat weightily on the state's coffers
Filling his wide mouth with all ten toes
Stuffing the imagined belly of the yet unborn blood
Till this sky could not contain his sleaze
And his graft goes global
Now he has fouled family and forth
His hunted head in a lady's headgear
His name hastily stinking homeward like a month's carcass
Has no place of escape, save the septic swamp
And the skeletons he created who pall his repute
With placards of blemished picture
No to arrest, no to trial
No to court case
We no go gree ...

Tell me miracles

Tell me
    miracles, not magic, not staged voodoo
Tell me
    five loaves and two fishes for all
Tell me
    of dead Lazarus risen by pure prayers
Tell me
    of the truly blind that regains sights
Tell me
    miracles from pure breath to pristine firmament
Tell me
    miracles unrehearsed and right on point

Tell me
    miracles, not magic, not staged voodoo
Tell me not
    of decently dressed devil try at organized crusades
Tell me not
    of imported moneymaking ministers of gods
Tell me not
    of coming for my magic at matted school grounds
Tell me not
    of seasoned magic marketers in imposing galleries
Tell me not
    of conjured gibberish and abracadabra
Tell me not
    of seeking salvation at targeted chapels and crusades
Tell me no more
    'God has sent me to you'

Tell me
    miracles, not magic, not staged voodoo.

Idols on altars

We worshippers in feverish earnest
Reverent devotion to the altar our slogan
In fine fraud or infernal fun
Our altar the spiritual refuge
In farts or forced fulsome blood
Hurriedly to our waiting altars
Anointing fraud, fun, farts, and banned blood

Our pockets in reverent devotion
Always to the spiritual saliva
Of the requesting tongues of the demanding altar
And the anointed hands of the tithy ritual
Chained to our altars in sleek worship

Adorations to our heavily robed altars
Decent deities detesting kernel, gore from gored
Or *Èkuru* in sacrificial calabashes at crossroads
But offerings at weekly thanksgivings
Streams of civilised tenth at every turn our potion,
Compelled by the incisioned tongues
Plus singular obligation of ruinous blessings.

Altars of prayer bazaar for venal politicians,
Kind kidnappers and the most wanted
Most faithful depositors of wheels of ministration
Stolen or bloodstained treasures
The Lord and we love you all
And riches reek not of blood

Altars of golden evangelism on golden crafts
Flights of taxed fullness from Africa to Europe
On the wasted wings of the weakly wailing wretch
Wretch who wait ad nauseam on crumbling limbs

For promised miracles and wonders
Wretch fed a mite of magic
As the bounty of idolized altars in affluence
Jet set in golden jets of wretches' sweats

Hmmm! Now I see …
Ìgunnu belongs to the blind
The wise acolyte handles his treasury
As we shall take from the hoodwinked
So shall we give unto the rich sly altar

---

* *Èkuru:* a meal of peeled beans common among the Yoruba of
  West Africa.
* *Ìgunnu* or *Ìgunnukó*: a very long West African masquerade
  without apparent means of seeing and believed to have no means
  of knowing how much money his acolyte makes for him.

Booze thralldom

Drunks die not outdoors
slowly but surely, I'll arrive home
For a certainty, home is woodcock's end point.

but my sights are playing muddy pranks on me
Clearly lighted visions now and again darkly blurred
both hands involuntarily wiping my foreign face
frantically fingering out the foreign murk of blindness
my failed sights must be lighted up
For a certainty, home is woodcock's end point.

Drunks die not outdoors
slowly but surely, I'll arrive home

but my long lifelong limbs are failing me,
Calcified bones and trusted plasm of veins
Strong supports now dancing wobbly woefully
buckling, bending, warping and giving way
to the foreign light-heavy weight of liquor
aye! in million tumbles … my legs must cart me home
For a certainty, home is woodcock's end point.

Drunks die not outdoors
slowly but surely, I'll arrive home

but my paths are plotting against me
These paths I traversed in dull days of rain
In nasty nights of nocturnal prowlers
now spinning hard, hilly and bushy plans
to get me sapped, spent and sorely slogged
plot and connive, sap or slog me
Home calls and I come
For a certainty, home is woodcock's end point.

Drunks die not outdoors
slowly but surely, I'll arrive home

but my earth is holding my legs down
Soft surfaces smooth flatterers of my heels
now sand-duned, seizing deep my supple limbs
crippling irritations rearing my ride rearward
But rear homeward a boozer must!
For a certainty, home is woodcock's end point.

Drunks die not outdoors
slowly but surely, I'll arrive home

but home has pushed itself farther away from me
my trusted haven has conspired with the traitors:
my sights, limbs, paths and earth
A simple flight of some graceful breaths
turns a tough trudge of eternity
Conspire and toughen my trip, home is sure
For a certainty, home is woodcock's end point.

Drunks die not outdoors
slowly but surely, I'll arrive home

but oh! Warm spring streaming out my groin
soaking me loincloth-down-to-footing!
why would my bladder join the traitors!
I must drag on!
oh … hmmm … lost my … footing …
oh … the dirty dust of the disloyal earth cuddled me!
deep shit!
The reward roué reaps?
I must coax my limbs!
For a certainty, home is woodcock's end point.

Drunks die not outdoors
slowly but surely, I'll arrive home

call not a boozehound foolish
for he is only fritting away his wealth

Drunks die not outdoors
slowly but surely, I'll arrive home
For a certainty, home is woodcock's end point.

Song of the sadist

The powerful beyond my power
I deify with dressed deference
for the fury in their hands
I hate to taste.

The weak within my grasp
I harass to their humble knees
for the dominance I possess
I must play out.

Between the pain for the powerless
doled out by my dominant sense
and the pleasure for the powerful
supplied by my spineless sheep
lies my province of power.

Face the fowl ...

Stand up you

Stand up you
Who sat like a soaked loaf
Stand up for the name of this land
Which carved you from its crooked crock
Crock transforming your name:
Nonentity now known entity.

Stand up you
And raise your strident voices
Shout for the name of this spread
This snow which currently cleanses your hearts
To the wailing deluge of pure purity
Coming again, coming to cleanse the purloined estate.

Stand up you
And shed oceans of tepid tears
To shoo away they who bled the home of honour
To bleach away the red stains of oil,
Poured on this garment at the gallery.

Stand up you
Who learn the cuneiforms of sand
On the wide palms of this land
Who speak to the universe
On the shoulders of this estate
Who soar to satellites
On the airy wings of this ceaseless spread
Who sages and saints salute
For this earth is your garment
Stand up and breathe refinement into raw raiment.

Stand up you
Who fear the raw deal of terror

From raw dealers of death on savage streets of survival
For death deals from Botha to Madiba
Death deals from Nigerian juntas to Gani
Plucked out not a tress, not a strand
From the lofty ideals of legends.

Stand up you
Hunkering hearts and bent backbones
For if not your numbness in tongues and veins
If not this time when the buoyant house is hollow
Would lepers remove rags and fan sad skins
Walk elegantly left and low
Look blissfully at those sorry frames
And claim none is as fit?

Stand up you
For what manner of purification,
What waters from what scented oceans
Can scour the charcoal's vileness and dress it in white
What bleach can exorcise variations from chameleon's core.

Stand up you
For big skull answers not big brain
Big body opens not the door
Save the inheritor of the key
Big vestment makes not a truly big man.

Stand up you
Firm heights of experiences
Who hold the keys of harmonious headway
Stand up and wake your mute minds and listless limbs
To restore the radiant moon as right as rain.

Here

You are not here
This void where hostility is god
Here where bile in breasts is whitened with sweet smiles

Here to sweat and arc tilling the soil?
Here to munch and gulp wastes?
Here to fatten, fart and shine darkly?
Here to vomit obscenities and spread vain sprouts?
Here to wait, watch and wither?

You are not here
Until the human in you is spiritedly alive,
To mow down mushrooming monsters
Standing straight like okro stems
Taller than the farmers who sourced them.

You are not here
Until the human in you is aroused,
Awake to sweep away walking ills
From this stretch of splashing triad
And cleanse the streets of obscenities

You are not here
When your chauffeur
Embraces sleep at the wheel
And you back his right to sleep at will
The disaster in reckless sleep
Soon puts all to ghastly sleep

You are not lazily here,
Not lamely alive
Until shackled in tongue
Manacled in limbs,
Your soul proscribes these monsters

Your heart slings poisonous spikes of hate
At these forays of felons

You are not here
When stinks saturate your air
When dirt smacks your face
And you embrace dumbness and frailty
You are in the hereafter.

Successful

Successful is the owner of the white
Who measured materials for spouse, sons and daughters
Who cut fine fabrics for family, friends and foes
Who cut clean cloths for kings, queens and crown princes
Who clothed his servile self in spotless white
And the silvery sky smiles enviously
At the purity of the virgin touch of whites.

Morning dews washed his breasts white
As rain water washes impurities
His body and blood bow humbly to the
Rhythmic beatings of fulfilling atonement
The sun on his head arrayed in silvery smile
And the heavens shine a genial smile
And spread its white brocade on his path.

But the miserly, drunk with parsimony,
Swayed his cap of long stupidity
With his penny-pinching minuscule knuckles
To label the gesture a bleak waste
And the owner of the white cloth a profligate.

At the grand festival of honour
When all the earth was white
And heavens witnessed snowy garments
Of fine-drawn shapes for all sizes
Conferring success on the radiant skins
Beautified by stunning sizes and shapes of white.

The grand success for the owner of the white cloth
The beacon, the honour at the festival of Honour
As honour for the owner of the lone lamp
In that village of owlish night

Who freely lightens others' lamps
From his large lamp of success
And generously brightens hearts at nights.

Natal kneeling

Here it is like yesterday
When the belle, connubially claimed by the colossal Àjànò
Was ripe to drop the starry yam by nature's lease
From the floating warmth of her watery within.

Yeeeh! Alone on a glad darkly day like this!
Save for the evil ears of the dark eye
The evil of a saintly day!
That picked up the outcry after the painful pangs
Induced by the pressure from her inner warmth.

Sharp slaying spasms, inviters of distress above distress
And ... blacking out? ... and the outflow ... urine?
Oh! This doomed day?
Kneeling, crouching and discarding coverings ...
Nature's silent command braces up the belle.

Succour from behind she must render
So tradition commands
Death from behind she must dispense
So the nocturnal feathers decree
The owl held back ...
Thrilling her black heart with macabre music ...
This must fail ... this star, this meteor must fall ...

By nature's command the floating warmth
Reared infirm head through the slippery threshold
Expanding passage to the frosty sphere
Fortune is fated this day
The nocturnal wing pulled kneeling limbs from the rear
Tightly shutting down the earthly gate
Evil minds rendered wretched by wickedness
Incited from the rein of the reigning mandate

Kneeling natally, she cursed the owl!
Kneeling natally, she cursed the coven!
She cursed the black and red wings!

Heaven's palms at hand
Tornadoes of terror in haste
Dashing after the damned eye
Weakling in sight of saintly strength
Away the darkness fled!

Crossing the threshold of new life
And crying triumphantly,
The cherub arrived in blood
The belle glistened in blood and joy.

Born and ripened in this realm of crisis
We call this a child of crisis
Crisis strengthens this: in crisis you thrive.

---

* *Àjànọ* or *Àjànàkú*: a sobriquet for the elephant among the Yoruba.

The womb

See the watery warmth which wells up steadily
Nine-moons' swiveling voyage in the womb,

See that which courses causing no crack or crash
Is the supremacy of creation within creation

That which happens to tubers in pregnant heaps
And the ridges tear and crack a resounding crack

That which comes up in the busy wombs of factories
The killing noise of the blazing and grinding metals

That watery swell which weighs heavily on the sky
And wearily weeps down its bulging burden in torrents

That waste which the earth consumes of dirt and filth
And vomits in bouts of diarrheic earthquakes

That which the ocean shyly takes in to spacious womb
And presently pours forth in violent waves and surges

That burdensome joy only a womb can sustain
Is the nation of finest novelty moulded by Nature's hands

Wait on the womb! Deify the divine!

One white witch

White wings of shielding light,
Banisher of the poisonous wings of darkness
Flapping flagellums flying forever
In the snowy coven of silvery witchery.

Three lone long strands decking her chin
White locks so wizened with wisdom
Bulging eyes more penetrating than eagle's:
Her silent armours on hot grounds.

The utmost hunger to shield hers is the drive
Unleashing the potency of her white witchery to her will
On that voyage traverses only by the fittest of the dark
Fighting the nocturnal feathers in their darkly coven
Dark or red: the bitter donors of blood and death

She is the blindfolded, blinded who sees like the eagle
She is the roguishly rheumatised ray who flies moon-athon
She is the leaded heart who wields her wand of witchery
She is the slain and slain who stretches her soul aloft
She is the gleaming goddess who defies her foes' gaol
She is the precious gold who blinds the bleak sun from the
coven

'The hoary mother bewitched you,' the fortune-teller tattles.
'Yes, she cast her spell on me ... Let me be jinxed!
May I drink from her witches' brew over again.'

You are the white feathers, the hoary Mother
Who had vowed with her all to bewitch me
And now you did
I hold the wand of long life
I discern the lines on my palms
I fathom the tenor of the world

I stand sprightly tall in humility
The planet pays ears to my stirring lines
Heavens stamp my simple submissions
The witches' sabbaths sponsor the seeds I sow

A curse of sanity is placed on me
For continuous care is my seemly sacrifice for elders
May your hoary Mother curse you to sanity, torment you to
triumph
May your quest be charmed from ruin to renewal
When you have offered sacrifices in due measures:
Ample ransom of care and robust deference
Sacrifices tempting satiated eyes in heavens and earth
And the roof above and the mat underneath shall greet
Your servile self with quails and fruitage.

Said she

said she
to us little sons
destined to reach our summits we are
in our lost world
by our own makings

said she
to us lanky lads
designed to clinch our aspirations we are
in our selfish world
by our singular efforts

said she
to me solitary soul
be as large as elephant you shall
as nobly exalted as lion
in the sight of our world

if

rely on your palms
shun what the next soul holds
look up to the bounties of heavens
you will

Stumps

Morning ...
Woodcutter toiling
Success strides
Sweating saliva and spitting sputum

Snubbing stumps, the two-life cords
Youthful yesterday
But wrinkled today

Noon ...
Rippling muscles
Hard flesh and torn palms
Abating spirit

Dusk ...
Loaded: gold and honey
Name, fame, families
Life

Night ...
Two stumps, ancestral paths
Ignored stubs still wrinkling

Take-home ...
Tree falls here
Falls there
Full fall, all fall
Fall ... lost to stumps

Says the spirit

Like the drooping bat
The world droops down her head:
The towns are in turmoil
As priests anoint horrors
Hymn mores off the scriptures
Clear the paths to gory riches
Praise and pray the devil
Sail silently by thrashed truth
Flow with fuelled fantasies.

Like the drooping bat
The world droops down her head:
The towns are in turmoil
As mothers banish breasts
Tear tempting temples to tatters
Market promising morrows
Build brothels between buttocks
Mute minds as bizarre buyers break in.

When the world droops down her head
Like the drooping bat
When the towns are in turmoil
Ask the priests, the priests of possessions
The greedy wolfs heralded by the doves
The specious white that sell the pulpit for the shadows
The mouths that vomit the scriptural purity
At the faint fear of want
Ask the priests says the sagely spirit.

When the world droops down her head
Like the drooping bat
When the towns are in turmoil
Ask the mothers, the mothers who opened private doors

To strangers with pulsating veins of marijuana
Who borrowed morals from dogs and pigs
And bless broods with monkey's bare bottoms
Ask the mothers says the sagely spirit.

The journey

Is it a long journey?
From high roof to the sandy bed
Ask the swift tongues of blissful rain
Swift and smooth is the soggy descent.

Is it an extended excursion?
From this bed to the beyond
Ask the piercing ploughs of the earthworm
Sweet and brief is the burrowing fun.

Is it a distant drive?
From that tomb to the strange start
Ask your morbidly shrouded friend
Fast and certain is the return journey.

Life dialectics

Between sterile heavens and sullied spheres
    The rational but irrational hominids

Between cracking cries at *kneelings* and the closing lids and lips
    The tellurian span, short flash like a blink

Between penurious rights and richly wrapped wrongs
    The greedy jaws of cunning reptilian breeds

Between virgin dogma and golden voidness
    The strayed dogs deaf to the good hunter's hoots

Between tangy-tasting truth and sweetly scented spuriousness
    The vacillating minds of millions in ignorance

Between palms of green from the roof and constant ruin of the terrain
    The scorching groan under torn tent and over wrecked bed

Between the feral head of the West and the wisdom of the sage
    The hasty rush eternally sealing the madness of doomed conformists

Between the simple 'let there be still light' and the willfully noisy 'never!'
    The constant clashes of heaving hearts among cultures of actuality

Between the solemn study of the source and sensual materialism

The unviable longing to linger here fledgling fresh
forever

Between the short flash in the market and the certainty of
eonian homecoming
The irreversible reality of life lived right or wrong

Life is

that big black cauldron
of sweet, freshly simmered soup
teeming with tempting chunks of choice meat
small, sizeable, sumptuous and shapely
swimming within the juicy world of the wide pot,
the likes *Aṣọ ẹbi* eats at burial ceremonies.
Humans, the tempting chunks
before the painful poise of Death
who happily picks when and how He prefers
now, soon and again from the helpless pot
to quench His chronic cravings.

The bell

The bell clanks!
    'Clank clank!
This span!
    Span span!
Shall end!
    End end!
Cer tain
    Cer tain!'

Long bell clangs!
    'Clang clang!
This being!
    Being being!
Shall end!
    End end!
Fi nite!
    Fi nite!'

Sweet sorrow

So sweet, sweet nothings
From the Liberty road
To his confined bunk
Under his heaving reeks
One … two … three exhausted rounds.

So simple, so sweet
From bottomless pockets
To sweating palms
Of the fair lovely warmth
One … three … five crispy mints.

So sour, so stale
From sudden growth
To steady bloat
Of brazenly bulging shame
One … five … nine agonizing moons.

So sour, so sorrowful
From promising beauty
To ragged reject
In the world once loving
Before … now … forever shameful life.

Your planet

From it you won fresh life
You won tender warmth
You won brains and strength
You till your sweet victuals in sweat

      In it you tarry for a term
      You seek soothing balm
      You mushroom in wet and warm
      You soon wear out like the dry weather

            In it you grow gaunt and sluggish
            You lean on hands for help
            You sleep to wake another day
            You hate to wait for the last exit

                But you surely know the exit calls.

Kraftgriots

Also in the series (POETRY) *continued*

Joe Ushie: *A Reign of Locusts* (2004)
Paulina Mabayoje: *The Colours of Sunset* (2004)
Segun Adekoya: *Guinea Bites and Sahel Blues* (2004)
Ebi Yeibo: *Maiden Lines* (2004)
Barine Ngaage: *Rhythms of Crisis* (2004)
Funso Aiyejina: *I,The Supreme & Other Poems* (2004)
'Lere Oladitan: *Boolekaja: Lagos Poems 1* (2005)
Seyi Adigun: *Bard on the Shore* (2005)
Famous Dakolo: *A Letter to Flora* (2005)
Olawale Durojaiye: *An African Night* (2005)
G. 'Ebinyo Ogbowei: *let the honey run & other poems* (2005)
Joe Ushie: *Popular Stand & Other Poems* (2005)
Gbemisola Adeoti: *Naked Soles* (2005)
Aj. Dagga Tolar: *This Country is not a Poem* (2005)
Tunde Adeniran: *Labyrinthine Ways* (2006)
Sophia Obi: *Tears in a Basket* (2006)
Tonyo Biriabebe: *Undercurrents* (2006)
Ademola O. Dasylva: *Songs of Odamolugbe* (2006), winner, 2006 ANA/Cadbury
    poetry prize
George Ehusani: *Flames of Truth* (2006)
Abubakar Gimba: *This Land of Ours* (2006)
G. 'Ebinyo Ogbowei: *the heedless ballot box* (2006)
Hyginus Ekwuazi: *Love Apart* (2006), winner, 2007 ANA/NDDC Gabriel Okara
    poetry prize and winner, 2007 ANA/Cadbury poetry prize
Abubakar Gimba: *Inner Rumblings* (2006)
Albert Otto: *Letters from the Earth* (2007)
Aj. Dagga Tolar: *Darkwaters Drunkard* (2007)
Idris Okpanachi: *The Eaters of the Living* (2007), winner, 2008 ANA/Cadbury
    poetry prize
Tubal-Cain: *Mystery in Our Stream* (2007), winner, 2006 ANA/NDDC Gabriel
    Okara poetry prize
John Iwuh: *Ashes & Daydreams* (2007)
Sola Owonibi: *Chants to the Ancestors* (2007)
Adewale Aderinale: *The Authentic* (2007)
Ebi Yeibo: *The Forbidden Tongue* (2007)
Doutimi Kpakiama: *Salute to our Mangrove Giants* (2008)
Halima M. Usman: *Spellbound* (2008)
Hyginus Ekwuazi: *Dawn Into Moonlight: All Around Me Dawning* (2008), winner,
    2008 ANA/NDDC Gabriel Okara poetry prize
Ismail Bala Garba & Abdullahi Ismaila (eds.): *Pyramids: An Anthology of Poems
    from Northern Nigeria* (2008)
Denja Abdullahi: *Abuja Nunyi (This is Abuja)* (2008)
Japhet Adeneye: *Poems for Teenagers* (2008)

Seyi Hodonu: *A Tale of Two in Time (Letters to Susan)* (2008)
Ibukun Babarinde: *Running Splash of Rust and Gold* (2008)
Chris Ngozi Nkoro: *Trails of a Distance* (2008)
Tunde Adeniran: *Beyond Finalities* (2008)
Abba Abdulkareem: *A Bard's Balderdash* (2008)
Ifeanyi D. Ogbonnaya: *... And Pigs Shall Become House Cleaners* (2008)
Ebinyo Ogbowei: *the town crier's song* (2009)
Ebinyo Ogbowei: *song of a dying river* (2009)
Sophia Obi-Apoko: *Floating Snags* (2009)
Akachi Adimora-Ezeigbo: *Heart Songs* (2009), winner, 2009 ANA/Cadbury poetry
    prize
Hyginus Ekwuazi: *The Monkey's Eyes* (2009)
Seyi Adigun: *Prayer for the Mwalimu* (2009)
Faith A. Brown: *Endless Season* (2009)
B.M. Dzukogi: *Midnight Lamp* (2009)
B.M. Dzukogi: *These Last Tears* (2009)
Chimezie Ezechukwu: *The Nightingale* (2009)
Ummi Kaltume Abdullahi: *Tiny Fingers* (2009)
Ismaila Bala & Ahmed Maiwada (eds.): *Fireflies: An Anthology of New Nigerian
    Poetry* (2009)
Eugenia Abu: *Don't Look at Me Like That* (2009)
Data Osa Don-Pedro: *You Are Gold and Other Poems* (2009)
Sam Omatseye: *Mandela's Bones and Other Poems* (2009)
Sam Omatseye: *Dear Baby Ramatu* (2009)
C.O. Iyimoga: *Fragments in the Air* (2010)
Bose Ayeni-Tsevende: *Streams* (2010)
Seyi Hodonu: *Songs from My Mother's Heart (2010),* winner ANA/NDDC Gabriel
    Okara poetry prize, 2010
Akachi Adimora-Ezeigbo: *Waiting for Dawn* (2010)
Hyginus Ekwuazi: *That Other Country* (2010), winner, ANA/Cadbury poetry prize,
    2010
Emmanuel Frank-Opigo: *Masks and Facades* (2010)
Tosin Otitoju: *Comrade* (2010)
Arnold Udoka: *Poems Across Borders* (2010)
Arnold Udoka: *The Gods Are So Silent & Other Poems* (2010)
Abubakar Othman: *The Passions of Cupid* (2010)
Okinba Launko: *Dream-Seeker on Divining Chain* (2010)
'kufre ekanem: *the ant eaters* (2010)
McNezer Fasehun: *Ever Had a Dear Sister* (2010)
Baba S. Umar: *A Portrait of My People* (2010)
Gimba Kakanda: *Safari Pants* (2010)
Sam Omatseye: *Lion Wind & Other Poems* (2011)
Ify Omalicha: *Now that Dreams are Born* (2011)
Karo Okokoh: *Souls of a Troubadour* (2011)
Ada Onyebuenyi, Chris Ngozi Nkoro, Ebere Chukwu (eds): *Uto Nka: An Anthology
    of Literature for Fresh Voices* (2011)
Mabel Osakwe: *Desert Songs of Bloom* (2011)
Pious Okoro: *Vultures of Fortune & Other Poems* (2011)

Godwin Yina: *Clouds of Sorrows* (2011)
Nnimmo Bassey: *I Will Not Dance to Your Beat* (2011)
Denja Abdullahi: *A Thousand Years of Thirst* (2011)
Enoch Ojotisa: *Commoner's Speech* (2011)
Rowland Timi Kpakiama: *Bees and Beetles* (2011)
Niyi Osundare: *Random Blues* (2011)
Lawrence Ogbo Ugwuanyi: *Let Them Not Run* (2011)
Saddiq M. Dzukogi: *Canvas* (2011)
Arnold Udoka: *Running with My Rivers* (2011)
Olusanya Bamidele: *Erased Without a Trace* (2011)
Olufolake Jegede: *Treasure Pods* (2012)
Karo Okokoh: *Songs of a Griot* (2012), winner. ANA/NDDC Gabriel Okara
     poetry prize, 2012
Musa Idris Okpanachi: *From the Margins of Paradise* (2012)
John Martins Agba: *The Fiend and Other Poems* (2012)
Sunnie Ododo: *Broken Pitchers* (2012)
'Kunmi Adeoti: *Epileptic City* (2012)
Ibiwari Ikiriko: *Oily Tears of the Delta* (2012)
Bala Dalhatu: *Moonlights* (2012)
Karo Okokoh: *Manna for the Mind* (2012)
Chika O. Agbo: *The Fury of the Gods* (2012)
Emmanuel C. S. Ojukwu: *Beneath the Sagging Roof* (2012)
Amirikpa Oyigbenu: *Cascades and Flakes* (2012)
Ebi Yeibo: *Shadows of the Setting Sun* (2012)
Chikaoha Agoha: *Shreds of Thunder* (2012)
Mark Okorie: *Terror Verses* (2012)
Clemmy Igwebike-Ossi: *Daisies in the Desert* (2012)
Idris Amali: *Back Again (At the Foothills of Greed)* (2012)
A.N. Akwanya: *Visitant on Tiptoe* (2012)
Akachi Adimora-Ezeigbo: *Dancing Masks* (2013)
Chinazo-Bertrand Okeomah: *Furnace of Passion* (2013)
g'ebinyŏ ogbowei: *marsh boy and other poems* (2013)
Ifeoma Chinwuba: *African Romance* (2013)
Remi Raji: *Sea of my Mind* (2013)
Francis Odinya: *Never Cry Again in Babylon* (2013)
Immanuel Unekwuojo Ogu: *Musings of a Pilgrim* (2013)
Khabyr Fasasi: *Tongues of Warning* (2013)
J.C.P. Christopher: *Salient Whispers* (2014)
Paul T. Liam: *Saint Sha'Ade and Other Poems* (2014)
Joy Nwiyi: *Burning Bottom* (2014)
R. Adebayo Lawal: *Melodreams* (2014)
R. Adebayo Lawal: *Music of the Muezzin* (2014)
Idris Amali: *Efeega: War of Ants* (2014)
Samuel Onungwe: *Tantrums of A King* (2014)
Bizuum G. Yadok: *Echoes of the Plateau* (2014)
Abubakar Othman: *Bloodstreams in the Desert* (2014)
rome aboh: *a torrent of terror* (2014)

Udenta O. Udenta: *37 Seasons Before the Tornado* (2015)
Magnus Abraham-Dukuma: *Dreams from the Creek* (2015)
Christian Otobotekere: *The Sailor's Son 1* (2015)
Festus Okwekwe: *Our Mother Is Not A Woman* (2015)
Tanure Ojaide: *The Tale of the Harmattan* (2015)
Chris Anyokwu: *Naked Truth* (2015)

Printed in the United States
By Bookmasters